TOWER HILL PAGEANT

Welcome to Tower Hill Pageant, London's first time ride museum. Here the city's exciting past is brought to life in an experience you won't forget.

AD 50

Roman Story

Within a few years of invading Britain in AD 43, the Romans built forts and towns across the conquered land, linked by a network of expertly built roads.

Some of these new roads had to cross the wide, tidal River Thames and within 50 years the first bridge was built. The army surveyors and engineers had to select their crossing point carefully. The south bank was generally marshy, but they made construction easier by choosing a point that had islands of solid ground.

On the opposite side, the north bank rose into two low hills, divided by a stream (later called the Walbrook). These hills formed the highest, driest site on the tidal river. A city soon took shape here, known to the Romans as Londinium.

Londinium soon became a thriving port with new timber quays and riverside warehouses. Food and wine, pottery,

A pottery oil lamp made near Lyons, France c. AD 200.

c.50

glass and other goods were shipped in from all parts of the Roman Empire.

Ships sailing in from the North Sea and the Channel tied up alongside local barges carrying building materials up and down the Thames. Many of the goods unloaded at these quays continued their journey by road to other parts of Roman Britain (Britannia), the first capital of which was at Colchester. But because of good communications the provincial government soon moved to Londinium.

Although further quays were built, the port was in decline by the middle of the 3rd century and it eventually lost its reputation as a major trading centre. It became walled, defensive, and much less populated. Then, in AD 410, as European tribes threatened the very heart of their empire, the Romans pulled out of Britain altogether and the city was left abandoned.

The landscape that greeted the Romans now lies deep beneath the city's streets. The ground level has risen by up to eight metres as, until recently, new buildings were built on the rubble of the old.

To find out what lies below the modern surface, archaeologists probe down with a special tool called an auger. It extracts a sample of material which reveals how deep the man-made layers go, and what lies beneath them. Using samples from a wide area of the city it is possible to map the contours of 2,000 years ago.

c.100

AD650

Saxon Lundenwic

For 200 years london lay abandoned. All that was to remain were the old city walls. Saxons from northern Germany settled in eastern England and eventually, after about AD 600, established a new town to the west of Roman Londinium. They spoke an early form of English and called their town Lundenwic – 'London port'. Modern names have provided clues to its location. Aldwych, a bustling street north of the Strand, is Old English for 'the old port' (the modern name was given after the old port was abandoned). The Strand itself was 'the beach' where ships were landed.

The Strand was ideal for the way these people lived and traded. Instead of the quays, warehouses and market squares of the Romans, they only needed a sloping foreshore where their ships could beach. Goods were sold straight from the boats. As well as local produce, there were shipments from farther afield. Merchants from the Low Countries brought German wine, pottery and millstones, taking back with them the woollen cloth produced in many Saxon homes. Some other seafarers were less welcome – Vikings from Norway and Denmark.

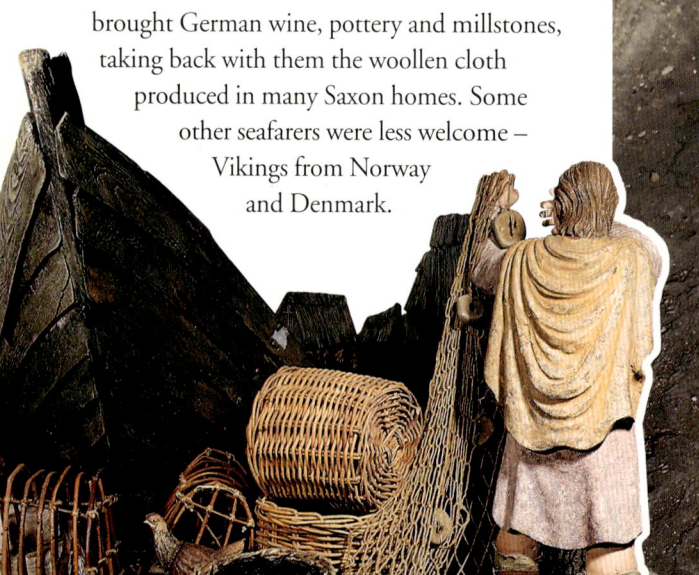

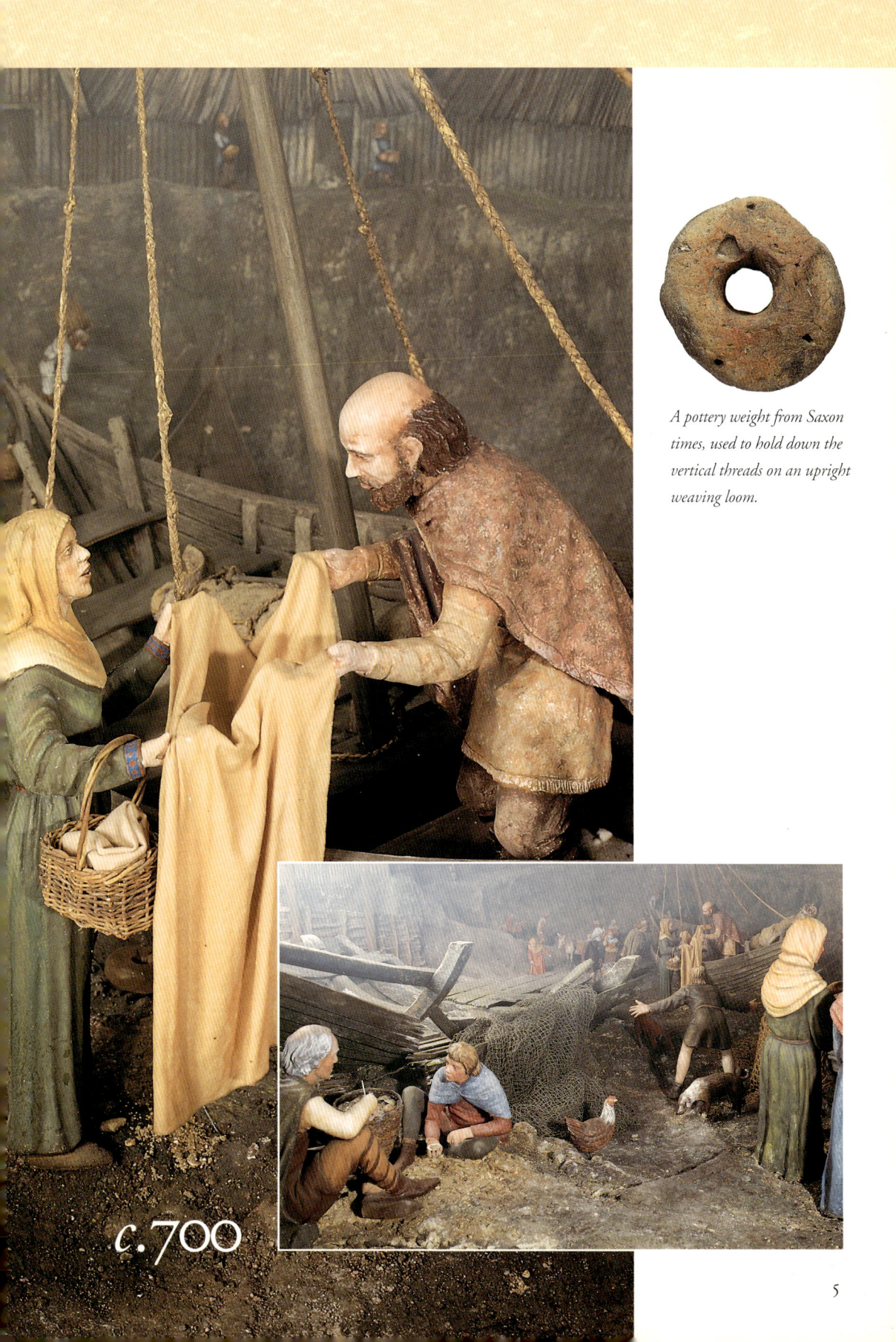

A pottery weight from Saxon times, used to hold down the vertical threads on an upright weaving loom.

c.700

AD 842

VIKING RAIDERS

LUNDENWIC, THE SAXON SETTLEMENT ALONG THE STRAND, WAS DEFENCELESS AGAINST THE VIKINGS. A raid in AD 842 caused 'great slaughter' according to a writer of the time, and after a number of similar attacks, the English King Alfred moved the population within the Roman walls for safety. After about 886, new streets were laid out and trade began again within the city walls. Between 954 and 1016 Saxon Londoners defended their new city against a second wave of Viking attacks. In one attempt in late 1009, a young Norwegian named Olaf Haraldsson set up camp across the river in Southwark. His men besieged the city for several weeks but 'always suffered damage there', as an English chronicler noted with satisfaction. Yet London could not hold out alone when the Danish King Cnut (Canute) conquered the rest of England in 1016. Though Cnut failed to take it by force, the city later surrendered to him. Fifty years after that, it was to surrender to another conqueror, William of Normandy.

A silver penny of King Alfred the Great, c.886, probably minted in London to celebrate his success against Viking invaders.

c.1009

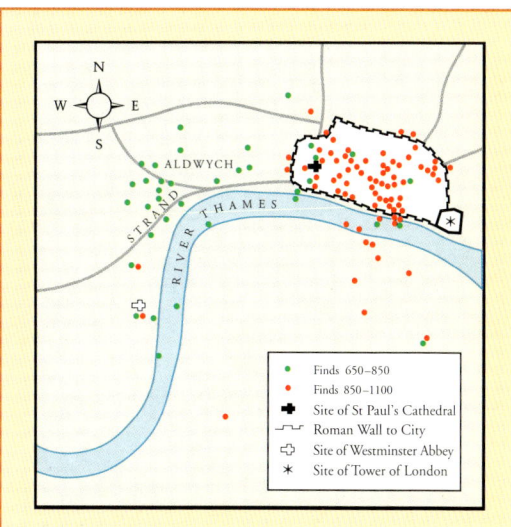

This map shows the site of archaeological finds from the Saxon period AD 650–850 (in green) and the later period, AD 850–1100 (in red). It shows very clearly that the first Saxons built their port around the Aldwych ('the old port') area west of the Roman city walls. In later years, when Viking longships became a constant threat up the river, Saxons built new homes behind the walls of the old city.

London's waterfront buildings are all located on land reclaimed from the Thames. The natural bank that the Romans first built on (A) is 100 metres away from today's river wall (B). Between these two points archaeologists have discovered an impressive number of Roman quays and medieval river walls built to stop erosion, for mooring ships, or to add a few metres to someone's backyard. A rich hoard of medieval finds has come from rubbish dumped as in-fill behind the wooden walls (revetments) which created each new extension. These riverside rubbish dumps soon became waterlogged and, without oxygen, the dumped objects did not rust or rot away.

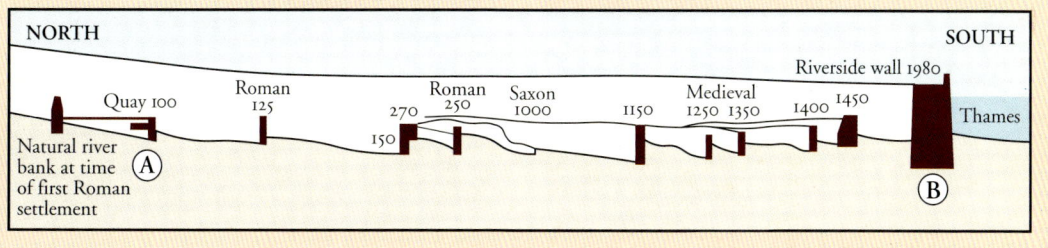

1066

The Norman Invasion

By the 11th century the long period of Saxon rule was nearing its end. After the death of the Dane Harthacnut in 1042 the English royal succession was no longer clear. After Edward the Confessor's death it was even less certain.

The pattern of London's growth was more clearly defined. There were many new streets and a new bridge at the same place as the old Roman crossing. New quays had been built on the river and, after three Danish kings, new trading links with Scandinavia had been established.

A development during King Edward's reign was destined to shape London's future. Edward was a religious man, as his nickname 'The Confessor' (meaning 'the priest') suggests. He poured untold wealth into the foundation of a great abbey on a marshy island to the west of the city. The church gave the district a new name – West Minster (west monastery) – and developed into today's Westminster Abbey. Next to his church, Edward built a palace which was to be the centre of his administration. This area is now occupied by the Houses of Parliament. So by 1066 the mould of present-day London was cast – finance in the city, government in Westminster.

The Norman invasion of that famous year did nothing to alter this trend. In fact William the Conqueror, like Harold, his slain predecessor, was crowned at Westminster Abbey to strengthen his hold on the succession. The need to control the chief city of his new realm led William to make his contribution to the London landscape. The Saxon Londoners were reluctant to accept William as their king, so the Conqueror decreed that amongst many fortresses built throughout the land, no less than three castles were to be built in London. Two near St Paul's have disappeared

A child's shoe from the Norman period. Made of leather, it has a drawstring to fasten it around the ankle.

c.1066

The Bayeux Tapestry depicts William I's invasion. Below, a silver penny shows him with crown and sceptre.

almost without trace; the other remains world famous – the Tower of London.

Archaeological and documentary evidence of Norman London is plentiful and detailed. William I's famous Domesday Book survey of 1086 indicates that Greater London was dotted with fields, farms, mills and fisheries. In 1173 a writer describes in glowing terms the many features of the Norman city – its sturdy walls and gates, fine parish churches, great monasteries and hospitals. It was, he said, 'the most noble city'.

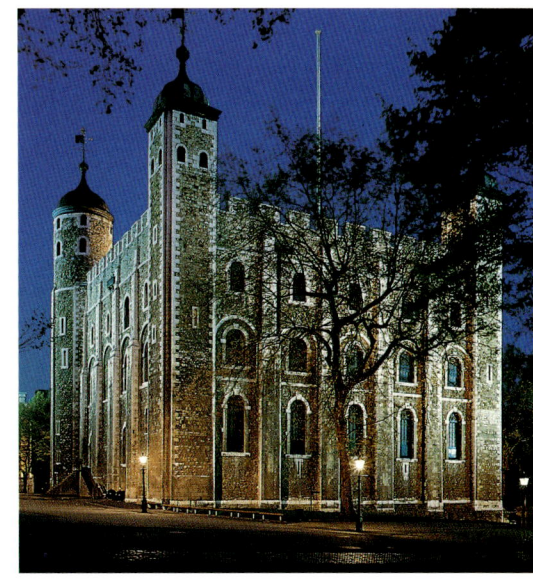

1250

Medieval Trade

After the Norman Conquest, the city waterfront developed into a cosmopolitan port with impressive warehouse facilities. At the eastern end was the great castle begun by William the Conqueror, the Tower of London. A wide range of imports arrived at the main public quays, Queenhithe and Billingsgate. The chief exports, wool and woollen cloth, were handled at Custom House, where taxes were collected on them. Much of medieval London's trade was in the hands of powerful overseas merchants. The German Hanseatic League, which dominated North Sea commerce, had its own special quay and guildhall. Nearby was the wine quay, 'the Vintry', where barrels of Bordeaux wine came ashore. As well as the merchants themselves, there were now clerks to help with the accounts and teams of porters for the heavy work.

The Thames meant more to medieval Londoners than just ships and trade. Many depended on it for drinking water and for washing clothes. Dozens of narrow lanes ran down to the waterfront from Thames Street.

Merchants, fishmongers, cloth dyers, brewers and others lived along and between these lanes. They sometimes made it difficult for other people to get through by extending their houses into the street or by setting out stalls. Some even tried to charge the public for using 'their' lanes.

The lanes were supposed to be wide enough for two carts to pass, but many were not. With timber-framed buildings so closely packed along the waterfront, fire was a constant threat.

A 14th-century floor tile.

The lead seals commonly found along the waterfront recall one of medieval London's most important exports – woollen cloth. The quality of this cloth was strictly controlled. It was inspected and taxed by royal officials who fixed seals – such as those shown below – onto all the cloths which they passed.

The lettering and designs on the seals show that cloths made in many parts of the country were brought to London for finishing and export. Some were dyed here, seals from later periods occasionally referring to dyehouses by the Thames.

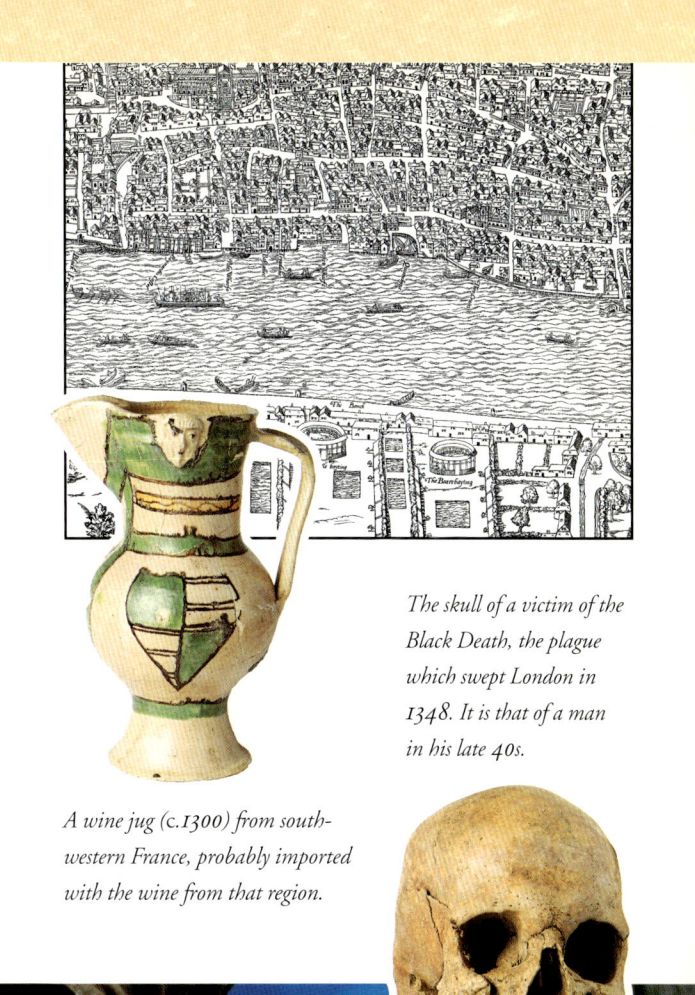

A wine jug (c.1300) from south-western France, probably imported with the wine from that region.

The skull of a victim of the Black Death, the plague which swept London in 1348. It is that of a man in his late 40s.

c.1400

1500
Tudor Trade

To the Londoner of Tudor times the capital must have seemed like three cities rather than one. To the west was a fashionable suburb of fine houses reaching along the Strand towards Westminster, home of the sovereign and parliament. In these new grand homes lived the élite – landed gentry, wealthy lawyers, high ranking government officials.

Directly south across the first stone London bridge was Southwark, a thriving suburb with great entertainment venues like the Globe Theatre.

But London's hub was still the old city within the Roman walls, where rich aldermen and paupers lived cheek by jowl. This was the commercial heart of city and nation, the engine room of enterprise. Commerce had never been more prosperous, for shipowners were quick to exploit trade with exotic lands opened up by daring explorers of the times.

In Tudor times London firmly established itself as Britain's largest port. Queenhithe and Billingsgate were still the main city quays, but ships bound for farther flung destinations now tied up at new berths downstream.

It was during this era that merchants first formed companies to foster and widen London's international trade. The East India Company, founded in 1600, was one of the most famous. The London guilds, set up in medieval times to control their trades – vintners, weavers, plumbers, goldsmiths and many others – prospered as never before, with fine halls dotted all over the city.

Gilded blue glass, probably from a wine goblet made in Venice.

Below right, an artist's impression of late medieval London.

c.1600

1665

The Great Plague

In the 1550s the population of the walled city and its suburbs was about 120,000. By 1660, it had reached 450,000. The medieval city was chronically overcrowded. Into its densely packed streets and alleys the sun rarely shone, fresh air rarely flowed. There were no drains and the water was often foul. In short, the place was a perfect breeding ground for disease.

The worst type of epidemic was the bubonic plague, an acutely infectious bacterium carried by rats and the fleas that fed on them. Its victims would first notice buboes, swellings in the armpit or groin. After that would follow chills, fever, vomiting, diarrhoea – and death.

There had been plagues in the city before: the Black Death in 1348 and an outbreak in 1563 which killed over 30,000. But the Great Plague of 1665/66 was the last and worst.

The epidemic began in the city in April 1665, brought in by rats from foreign cargoes. For 18 months,

Burial of victims of the Great Plague in a cemetery outside the city walls. Taken from an illustrated broadsheet of 1665 which records the number of deaths in each London parish during a single week.

London's First Stone Bridge – a 1630 view

Until the late 12th century, all the bridges that crossed the Thames were made of wood. Repairs were constantly necessary as storms and tides took their toll. In 1176, the decision was made to build a new bridge made of stone. It took 33 years to finish, had 19 arches and a wooden drawbridge to protect the city from attacks coming from the south. In the centre was a chapel and the gatehouse at the south end was surmounted by poles bearing the heads of traitors. In later years the bridge became tightly packed with shops and houses – 198 of them by the mid 14th century. This left a thoroughfare only three metres wide in places. Such was the congestion that boatmen still made a good living from rowing people across the river. This view by Claude de Jongh was painted in 1630. The buildings began to be removed in 1759 and the main structure was replaced in 1830.

a cross on a household door became a grimly familiar sight, warning those who sought to enter that the disease had visited before them. The dark streets echoed with the ring of the handbell, the sombre cry 'Bring out your dead' and the clatter of cartwheels as the bodies were borne away to be buried in mass graves outside the city walls. By the autumn of 1666 more than 80,000 people had perished.

But Lord! what a sad time it is to see no boats upon the River; and grass grows all up and down White Hall Court.

Samuel Pepys, 20 September 1665

1666
THE GREAT FIRE

The Monument, built by Wren between 1671 and 1677, to commemorate the Great Fire at the place where it started.

JUST ONE YEAR AFTER THE GREAT PLAGUE KILLED TENS OF THOUSANDS OF LONDONERS, THE CITY FACED ANOTHER DISASTER. In the early hours of Sunday 2 September 1666, a fire started in a bakehouse in Pudding Lane. After a long, hot summer everything in the city was tinder dry.

At first, few thought the flames would spread, but a strong easterly wind sent them roaring through the timber buildings of the waterfront, packed with inflammable goods, timber, pitch (wood tar) and oil. (In 1979, 20 charred barrels covered in pitch were found near Pudding Lane in the cellar of a building which had burned down, probably in the Great Fire.)

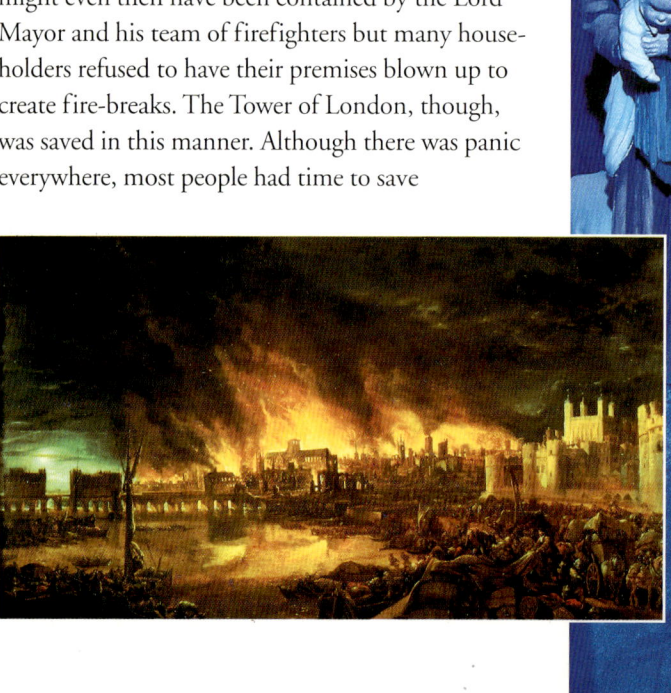

Soon the east wind drove the flames into the rest of the city. All Monday and Tuesday the wind blew and the fire gained momentum. The situation might even then have been contained by the Lord Mayor and his team of firefighters but many householders refused to have their premises blown up to create fire-breaks. The Tower of London, though, was saved in this manner. Although there was panic everywhere, most people had time to save themselves and whatever belongings they could carry on foot, by road or by river.

Mercifully, on Tuesday night the wind dropped. Gradually the blaze was controlled. By Thursday the exhausted citizens were able to survey the damage. The king addressed the refugees gathered on Moorfields, and assured them that the fire had not been started by religious extremists or hostile foreigners: it was simply an accident. Nevertheless, the city and its waterfront was reduced to rubble. Old St Paul's Cathedral was a smoking ruin. A total of 52 company halls, 87 churches and over 13,000 houses had been destroyed.

1666

1667
Rebuilding the City

Rebuilding the city after the great fire seemed an impossible task. Surveyors estimated the loss at £10,000,000 – at a time when the city's annual income was £12,000.

Yet despite these enormous costs, there were many positive aspects to the situation. London before the fire had been ugly, overcrowded and insanitary. The acres of wasteland left by the fire gave planners and architects the opportunity to build a radically new city.

In 1667 work began, overseen by six commissioners appointed by the Corporation of London. As the ownership of land and property was so complex, the commissioners kept the general pattern of the medieval streets, but made them broader and easier for traffic. New building laws were introduced. Timber was forbidden; brick or stone became compulsory. The size of buildings was strictly controlled. Wherever possible, individuals and companies had to fund their own rebuilding. A tax on coal raised £736,000 for the public works programme. This included road

A view towards the city by Canaletto (c.1750) showing Wren's many spires and his masterpiece, St Paul's Cathedral.

c.1670

improvements, extensions to the Thames quay and the rebuilding of the Guildhall and some of the 87 lost parish churches.

The dominant figure in the city's rebirth was Sir Christopher Wren. All 51 of its new churches were designed by him, as was the crowning glory of the new city, St Paul's Cathedral. Wren (1632–1723) was a remarkable man with a powerful personality. A distinguished mathematician and astronomer in his early years, he had only turned to architecture at the age of 29. In 1662 he was asked to consider improvements to old St Paul's.

But the Great Fire four years later presented him with an unexpected opportunity big enough to match his genius.

The speed of London's rebuilding was as remarkable as its quality. By 1671, 9,000 new houses and some of the major public buildings had been completed. By 1675, only nine short years after that fateful Sunday in Pudding Lane, most of the elegant new city was in place. London emerged triumphantly out of this disaster as a capital which could match the elegance of any other European city.

Right, a detail from Sir Christopher Wren's plans for the church of St Mary-le-Bow.

1700
Coffee Houses to Finance Houses

BY THE EARLY 18TH CENTURY, LONDON WAS GROWING INTO A CENTRE FOR MERCHANTS, BANKERS, SHIP OWNERS AND INSURERS. They met in coffee houses to drink, smoke and carry out their daily business. As the value and volume of trade increased, so did the sums of money involved. Some of the leading coffee houses, like Lloyds and Garraways, developed into

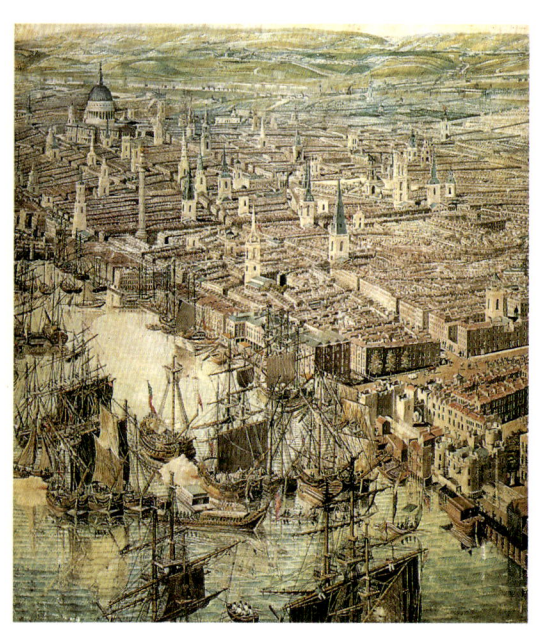

This section of the Rheinbeck Panorama (c.1820) shows the crowded Thames below London Bridge. Above the bridge, lighters, ferries and barges carried people and goods upstream.

Inside view of the modern Lloyds building, where the famous London underwriters are based.

the great insurance and finance houses which still dominate the city today.

Some of the coffee houses also served as sale rooms, where goods stored in the riverside warehouses were auctioned. To start one of these auctions, a short length of candle was lit. Bidding closed when the flame went out. Not all the goods bought in London were destined for the capital's own growing consumer market, or even for the rest of Britain. Many were reloaded on to ships bound, perhaps, for Europe or the American colonies.

Between 1700 and 1800 London's port became so busy that it was nearly choked by its own success. The number of ships bringing cargoes to London doubled. At the same time, ships were getting larger, so that the quantity of goods coming in went up fourfold. By law, many of these goods could only come ashore at the Legal Quays – 20 crowded wharves strung between London Bridge and the Tower. Larger ships moored down as far as Greenwich, but their cargoes could not avoid the Legal Quays. They had to be transferred on to barges for the short trip up to the city.

Doing business in a London coffee house. This cartoon first appeared in Every Man's Magazine *in 1772.*

c.1750

1900

The Growing Port

By 1900 London, at the heart of the vast British Empire, grew into the largest port the world had ever seen. London's dock system stretched 25 miles down the Thames to Tilbury.

This phenomenal expansion was initiated by the merchants themselves, who were losing millions through theft and delays caused by overcrowding. With the new docks downstream came huge new fortress warehouses. Here, even the largest ships could be unloaded quickly and securely. The West India Docks were the first to be built away from the city, opened in 1802 by merchants trading in Caribbean sugar and rum.

c.1890

The newly built West India Docks; an aquatint of 1802 by William Daniell.

At first the new docks took business away from the city waterfront, with most of the valuable and exotic goods coming in downstream.

Nevertheless, basic supplies like food and coal still came up to the city's wharves and, by 1850, their central location meant that they had won back much of the storage business from the docks. Huge new warehouses were built along Thames Street and across the river in Southwark. Barges were now free to go into the docks, and enormous quantities of tea, spices, rice and grain were transferred to warehouses lining both sides of the river. On the south bank, the stretch between London Bridge and Butler's Wharf became known as 'London's larder'.

New banks and offices opened in the city to service the port, and there was wealth to finance landmarks such as Tower Bridge, which opened in 1894. In the 1930s the docks employed 40,000 people, with as many again working on the river or at the wharves along its banks. Most of these were poorly paid casual labourers. Thousands of them waited at the dock gates each morning, hoping for a day's work.

23

1940

The Blitz and the Post War Years

The Thames brought trade and prosperity to London, but in late 1940 it also brought the bombers of the German Luftwaffe. Guided by the river, they bombed the capital every night for three months.

No one who lived through the Blitz could ever forget it. The docks and wharves were packed with raw materials for the war effort and supplies for

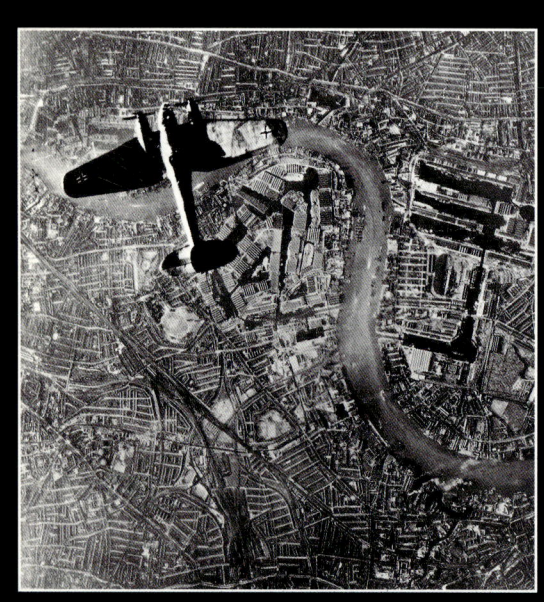

c.1940

A German Heinkel bomber over the East End. Tower Bridge is just visible on the left, casting shadows, and the dockland area, where the Canary Wharf buildings now stand, can be clearly seen on the right.

8 million Londoners. The East End became one of the most heavily bombed parts of Britain. Wartime fire-fighters faced some of the worst blazes the capital had seen since the Great Fire of 1666. Of the first night of the bombing, a former fireman gave this recollection: 'The high explosives and incendiary bombs had done their work. Huge fires were raging in the docks and in the factories lining the river banks … Flames were roaring from

lorries and trains. These developments, accentuated by strikes and poor labour relations, made the old docks redundant. Today's Port of London handles more cargo than ever before – but it is based at Tilbury, not in the city.

The Canary Wharf complex is the largest commercial development in Europe, the flagship of a massive regeneration programme for London's Docklands. Built on a peninsula known as the Isle of Dogs, three miles (five km) down river from Tower Bridge, it is on the site of the old West India Docks.

By the 1960s most of London's upstream docks were closed, overtaken by competition from larger, more modern European ports. Also gone were the dock industries. For years, huge areas of concrete and water lay derelict.

In 1981 the LDDC (The London Docklands Development Corporation) launched a development programme to breathe life into these wastelands. Public money created a new infrastructure – roads, sewers, a light railway linking Docklands to the city, with a new city airport nearby. Encouraged by tax incentives, private investment flowed in. Office blocks and new houses were built, old warehouses became desirable apartments. Shopping centres and recreational facilities followed. Although much remains to be done, a transformation is taking place.

timber yards, paint factories, soap works, sugar refineries, chemical works, dock warehouses and ships and the pathetic little homes of the workers.'

After the war the port soon recovered, though its days were numbered. In the 1960s there was a revolution in the way that goods were handled. Now they came packed in containers that could be loaded straight on to

The Waterfront Finds Museum

Tower Hill Pageant was entirely inspired by the wealth of finds unearthed on land reclaimed from the River Thames.

The Waterfront Finds Museum follows on from the time ride and presents a unique opportunity to view some of the discoveries made by Museum of London archaeologists.

A pottery spout from a bowl made in north-east France c. AD 150.

The museum is a complete attraction in its own right, and contains Roman and Medieval galleries. Together they contain over 1,000 artefacts and explain some of the evidence on which the time ride is based. Each section presents a different kind of find and a different technique of study.

On entering the museum, you will see a massive Roman quay found near London Bridge. Computer graphics show how this was built.

You will also walk through a full-scale reproduction of the Roman ship found at Blackfriars in the 1960s. The replica was made using original Roman techniques; a video shows how it was constructed, step by step.

In the adjoining gallery, the largest case contains parts of two wooden quay fronts, which protected

Remains of a man in his late 40s, a victim of the Black Death plague which devastated London in 1348.

the banks of the Thames in medieval times. These are now in air-conditioned showcases to prevent them from drying out.

Quaysides and Thames-side embankments were continually replaced in medieval London and the majority of the museum's artefacts were discovered behind such structures, including a dazzling array of medieval arts and crafts and a variety of medieval shoes.

Elsewhere in the museum you will see displays of pottery, documents, finds from the only Black Death cemetery known in Britain and lively presentations of how archaeologists examine and date their finds.

Not many people approve of new buildings in areas of historical or archaeological importance. But, without the construction of new office blocks along the Thames, little of the evidence would have been found and the Tower Hill Pageant story would have been incomplete.

Fragments of Roman pottery amphorae. These containers of olive oil, wine and many other foodstuffs were shipped into London from all over the Mediterranean.

Tower Hill Pageant

Tower Hill Pageant was made possible by recent archaeological discoveries beneath the streets of modern London. So it is fitting that the exhibition itself should be housed underground – in vaults beneath historic Tower Hill.

The vaults originally formed the basement levels of the Mazawattee Warehouse, a seven-storey eyesore built in 1864. The warehouse was erected on the site of medieval cottages belonging to the Royal Hospital of St Katharine by the Tower. It was not popular with local people. The Reverend Tubby Clayton, of neighbouring All Hallows Church, even nicknamed it the 'Nightmare of Tower Hill'. Perhaps his prayers were answered when the upper storeys were destroyed during the Blitz (although the vaults survived).

In more recent years, the vaults fell into disuse. Then, in 1987, the Culverin Consortium obtained a lease on the site from the Tower Hill Improvement Trust. The vaults were carefully restored, and opened to the public in 1991.

The Mazawattee warehouse decorated for the opening of Tower Bridge on 30 June 1894.

Construction work on the creation of Tower Hill Pageant (left) with, above, experimental work on a prototype of the time ride cars.